Henry Van Dyke

God and little children

The blessed state of all who die in childhood proved and taught as a part

of the gospel of Christ

Henry Van Dyke

God and little children
The blessed state of all who die in childhood proved and taught as a part of the gospel of Christ

ISBN/EAN: 9783337284329

Printed in Europe, USA, Canada, Australia, Japan

Cover: Foto ©Lupo / pixelio.de

More available books at **www.hansebooks.com**

GOD AND LITTLE CHILDREN:

THE BLESSED STATE OF ALL WHO DIE IN CHILDHOOD PROVED AND TAUGHT AS A PART OF THE GOSPEL OF CHRIST.

BY

HENRY VAN DYKE,

AUTHOR OF "THE REALITY OF RELIGION," "THE STORY OF THE PSALMS," ETC.

PUBLISHED BY ANSON D. F. RANDOLPH AND CO., 38 WEST TWENTY-THIRD STREET, NEW YORK.

To My Mother

IN MEMORY OF

HER CHILDREN IN HEAVEN

FROM ONE OF

HER CHILDREN ON EARTH

PREFACE.

These sermons were not written for the press, but for the pulpit, amid the incessant cares and labours of a pastor's life. Even for the correction of the manuscript and the reading of the proofs it has been necessary for me to rely on the kindness of friends, which I here acknowledge with gratitude.

The same reasons which led to the preaching of the sermons have made me consent to their printing, — a desire to bear strong and clear witness against a falsehood that has kept many men from loving God, and a still deeper desire to testify to the abundant grace of our Lord Jesus Christ as the Saviour of the world, and to bring a sure consolation to those who are in sorrow for the death of little children. The dark old dream of the perdition of infants has indeed begun to fade, long since, from the soul of Christendom, and the hope of their salvation has grown brighter and more clear from year to year; but there is still room and need for a book to prove that the black vision is utterly baseless, and that the bright hope is altogether reasonable, since it rests upon the same foundation as Christianity itself. And this, in brief, is what I desire to do: to show that

  NO CHILDREN LOST,
  ALL CHILDREN SAVED,

is as true as Gospel.

There are many things left out of this book for want of space. But one omission, I feel quite sure, will attract attention and comment. There is no attempt in these sermons to fix the age at which childhood ends and moral discretion begins. This omission is made on purpose, and simply because I do not know what that age is. Human laws recognize the distinction between childhood and maturity, but they differ greatly in the period at which they determine accountability. Indeed, it is hardly a matter which can be reckoned in years. And one thing is certain, — God will be not less, but more, just and merciful than man, in recognizing his little children and dealing gently with them, being mindful of their ignorance and weakness.

HENRY VAN DYKE.

New York City,
    Feb. 3, 1890.

THE INVISIBLE SERVICE

It is no little thing, when a fresh soul
And a fresh heart, with their unmeasured scope
For good, not gravitating earthward yet,
But circling in diviner periods,
Are sent into the world, — no little thing,
When this unbounded possibility
Into the outer silence is withdrawn;
Ah, in this world, where every guiding thread
Ends suddenly in the one sure centre, death,
The visionary hand of Might-have-been
Alone can fill Desire's cup to the brim!

How changed, dear friend, are thy part and thy
    child's!
He bends above thy cradle now, or holds
His warning finger out to be thy guide;
Thou art the nursling now; he watches thee
Slow learning, one by one, the secret things
Which are to him used sights of every day:
He smiles to see thy wondering glances con
The grass and pebbles of the spirit world,
To thee miraculous; and he will teach
Thy knees their due observances of prayer.

Children are God's apostles, day by day
Sent forth to preach of love, and hope, and peace;
Nor hath thy babe his mission left undone.
To me, at least, his going hence hath given
Serener thoughts and nearer to the skies,
And opened a new fountain in my heart
For thee, my friend, and all: and oh, if Death
More near approaches meditates, and clasps
Even now some dearer, more reluctant hand,
God, strengthen thou my faith, that I may see
That 't is thine angel, who, with loving haste,
Unto the service of the inner shrine
Doth waken thy beloved with a kiss.

JAMES RUSSELL LOWELL.

From Lines on the Death of a Friend's Child.

No Children Lost

I.

𝔄nd it came to pass, on the seventh day, that the child died. — 2 Sam. xii. 18.

AND then what became of the child? Whither did the young spirit fly? In what estate did the infant soul find itself when the last quivering breath had passed the lips and the tiny heart was lying still?

This is the question which rises to meet us at the death-bed of a child. It is the cry of the immortal love and tenderness by which God has bound the souls of parents to their children. David asked it in his grief three thousand years ago; and since then how many millions of men and women, looking down through their tears upon a silent little face, have murmured to themselves, "Where is my darling now?" Nor will it cease to be repeated while there is a true mother's heart beating in this world, or a father's spirit which retains one trace of the likeness of God's paternal love.

But we must not imagine for a moment that this question has no wider meaning, no weightier import, than that which is given to it by our personal affections. It is, in fact, one of the central questions of religion. It touches the justice and the goodness of the Divine Being. It affects more broadly than any other inquiry the ultimate destiny of the human race, of which the greater part dies in childhood. We are facing a question of immense importance when we ask what becomes of the little children when they die. It is time for us to take up the subject and consider it carefully. It is time for us to meet with candour the issues which are involved in it. It is time for us to go to the bottom of the subject, and make up our minds what the Word of God and the religion of Jesus Christ teach us to believe about it. And this is what I shall try to do, praying for light to discern the truth, and courage to speak it out, and skill to make it plain and straight and clear beyond the chance of mistake.

There are three, and only three, possible answers to the question, What becomes of those who die in infancy?

They are all lost.

Some of them are lost and some saved.

They are all saved.

The first answer we may pass without notice; for, so far as I know, it has never been accepted by Christian people, and it is not necessary for us to waste our time wandering in the absolute darkness of heathendom or materialism. The second answer, which divides the little children at death into two classes, and sends one class to heaven and the other class to hell, has undoubtedly been given by a great many people whose Christianity, to say the least, was sincere and honest. This is the doctrine which we shall consider in this sermon. I want to prove two things in regard to it: First, that it has been taught by men in almost every part of the Christian Church, from the fourth to the eighteenth century; Second, that it is certainly false, and that it is equally against reason and revelation to believe that there are any infants in hell.

I. It has been audaciously asserted and commonly believed that the doctrine of the perdition of infants originated with those theologians who are called Calvinists, and that the Presbyterian Church is peculiarly responsible for it. Never was there a more ignorant assertion, never an assumption more at variance with the facts.

It has been piously claimed, on the other hand, that the Calvinistic theology has never recognized this doctrine, and that the Presbyterian Church has kept itself entirely free from the shadow of it. Never was there a claim made with more amiable intentions and less substantial proofs.

The simple truth is, — and, after all, the truth is what we want, — that the responsibility for this doctrine rests, not upon any one branch of the Church, but upon theologians at large, from Saint Augustine down to the end of the seventeenth century. Here and there you will find men who were bold enough to deny and disavow it; but everywhere you will find men who not only accepted but taught it. That is the amazing fact. You will not discover those dreadful words, "Hell is paved with infants' skulls," in the works of any ancient writer. It is merely a waste of time to try to run that gray-headed falsehood to earth. But you will have no trouble in finding theories and statements which imply or declare that some infants pass through death into perdition, in the writings of Roman Catholics, Lutherans, Presbyterians, and Episcopalians.

Let us free our minds of cant; let us lay aside our prejudices, and examine the record fairly. You will naturally demand the proof of such a startling assertion, and you shall have it as briefly and as clearly as possible.

We may begin with Roman Catholic theologians. First comes St. Augustine, who was justly called *durus pater infantum*, — "the hard father of infants." He teaches that infants who die without baptism are lost; and though their punishment be of a milder sort than that of those who have added actual to original sin, they are finally excluded from the presence of God. Peter Lombard, in the twelfth century, puts the same doctrine very concisely when he says: "For original sin, which is derived from the parents, infants will be damned."[1] Tirinus, the Jesuit, writing in the seventeenth century, declares: " In the other life original sin —

---

[1] Lombard: Sentat. L. II. Quoted by Krauth: Infant Salvation, p. 68.

for example, in the case of infants who by it are unfitted for that life — is punished eternally; . . . they are in prison, light and pleasant indeed, yet of the nature of hell, in which, under the power of the Devil, they dwell to eternity." The canons of the Council of Trent, which still stand as an authoritative declaration of the faith of the Church, teach: "If any one denies that new-born children must be baptized, or says that they do not derive from Adam anything of original sin which makes the laver of regeneration necessary to cleanse them for an entrance into everlasting life, let him be accursed."[1] Such is the teaching of the Romish fathers.

Turn now to the Reformers. Take first the Augsburg Confession, drawn up by the

---

[1] Schaff: Creeds of Christendom, vol. ii. p. 86. See also the Roman Catechism, par. ii. cap. ii. Quæst. 25. "Unless they are born again by the divine grace of baptism, they are brought forth by their parents, whether they are believers or unbelievers, for eternal misery and perdition."

gentle Philip Melanchthon, — the earliest doctrinal statement of the Lutheran Church. It distinctly condemns all those who affirm that children may be saved without baptism: "Damnant Anabaptistas, qui improbant Baptismum puerorum, et affirmant pueros, sine Baptismo, salvos fieri."[1]

Following straight along this line we find the good Bishop Cranmer, of the English Church, saying in his Catechism: "If we should have heathen parents and die without baptism, we should be damned everlastingly." This was substantially the view of that branch of the Reformation which still held to sacramentarian doctrines and insisted upon baptismal regeneration. Turning to the other branch, we find its theologians asserting distinctly that infants may be saved without baptism. But on what ground? On the ground of a secret election of God which assigns some to heaven and others to hell.

Listen to John Calvin: "When the

[1] Confess. August., part i. art. ix.

Lord rejects the godless man, with his offspring, there is certainly no expostulation which we can make with God. . . . This, therefore, is to be held for certain, that all who are destitute of the grace of God are included under the sentence of eternal death; whence it follows that the children of the reprobate, whom the curse of God follows, are subject to the same sentence."[1] "Who will not adore this wonderful judgment of God, whereby it comes to pass that some are born at Jerusalem, whence they soon pass to a better life, while Sodom, the gate of the lower regions, receives others at their birth?"[2] "How comes it that the fall of Adam has involved so many nations, with their infant children, in eternal death, without remedy, unless because it pleased God? I confess that the decree is horrible; but none can deny that God foreknew the

---

[1] On Isaiah xiv. 21.
[2] J. Calvini Opera. Brunsvigæ, 1870. vol. viii. p. 309. De Æterna Dei Predestinatione.

end of every man before creating him, and foreknew it because he ordained it so." [1]

And then hear Cocceius of Holland and Molinæus of France, two great doctors of the seventeenth century: "Elect infants are not conceived and born as are the children of the Gentiles, concerning whom the presumption is certain that they with their mother's milk drink in godlessness unto destruction." [2] "As the eggs of the asp are deservedly crushed, and serpents just born are deservedly killed, though they have not yet poisoned any one with their bite, so infants are justly obnoxious to penalties." [3]

Finally, hear the Rev. Dr. Twiss, Prolocutor of the Westminster Assembly: "Many infants depart from this life in original sin, and consequently are condemned to eternal death on account of

---

[1] Instit., lib. iii. cap. xxiii. § 7.
[2] Catechis. Palat., Quæst. lxxiv.
[3] Anat. Arminianismi, p. 2.

original sin alone; therefore from the sole transgression of Adam condemnation to eternal death has followed upon many infants."[1]

But you are not to suppose that these teachings were confined to the books of divinity and sermons. They are to be found also in more popular literature. From this source we may take two characteristic examples. One is from the great Catholic poet Dante. He is entering the first circle of the Inferno; and there he hears the air trembling with the sighs of many infants and women and men. His guide says to him: —

> "Thou dost not ask
> What spirits these may be which thou beholdest:
> Now will I have thee know, ere thou go farther,
> That they sinned not; and if they merit had,
> 'T is not enough, because they had not Baptism,
> Which is the portal of the Faith thou holdest."[2]

The other is from a small Puritan poet, by name Michael Wigglesworth, of Massa-

---

[1] Vindiciæ, vol. i. p. 48.
[2] Inferno, book iv., Longfellow's Translation.

chusetts. He is describing the Last Judgment, and brings the reprobate infants before the bar of justice. They plead for pardon, but the Judge replies: —

> "You sinners are; and such a share
>   as sinners may expect,
> Such you shall have, for I do save
>   none but mine own Elect.
> Yet to compare your sin with their
>   who lived a longer time,
> I do confess, yours is much less,
>   though every sin's a crime.
> A Crime it is; therefore in bliss
>   you may not hope to dwell;
> But unto you I shall allow
>   the easiest room in Hell."[1]

Criticism upon these verses would be superfluous. But I think you will agree with me in saying that the man who could spend his time in carefully fitting such sentiments as these into a tripping metre and a double rhyme must have been a man, to use Dr. Johnson's phrase, "little to be envied."

"But for what reason," some one may

[1] The Day of Doom, 1662.

ask, "have you been at pains to collect these various and terrific utterances of so many men upon this subject?" There are two good reasons. First, in order to show clearly that this old doctrine of the perdition of infants is not a sectarian affair, not a thing to be treated as if it belonged to any particular age or any one set of Christians, but that the responsibility for it is very widely distributed, and that we are bound in honour to consider it in an atmosphere that is clear and free from all denominational bitterness and strife. Second, in order that we may understand clearly what it was that led men to hold and teach it. It was the subtle pride of intellect, the vain desire of absolute logical consistency. Starting with the most opposite premises, they felt bound to carry them out to the bitter end, no matter what it might be. Beginning, on the one hand, with the statement that baptism is absolutely necessary to salvation, they went straight on to the conclusion that unbaptized infants must be lost. Breaking away at the Reformation from that chain of error, they fell into another no less heavy, no less of iron. Setting out with the statement that God for his own glory predestines some men to everlasting death, they went straight on to the conclusion that the harmless, newborn children of Sodom are precipitated at death into perdition.

But were not the men who taught this great men, and learned men, and mighty men? Were they not very giants of logic, their little fingers thicker than the loins of the men of to-day? Yea, verily, and he would be over-bold who went out against them in his own strength. But do you remember another giant who stood forth as a champion, boasting that none could overthrow him? And do you remember a shepherd lad, who dared to face him with a sling and a smooth stone from the brook? There is an armoury which God has furnished for all who would withstand giants in His name. You may reach your hand down into the brook of living water that flows in the words of Jesus Christ. From those cool depths you take a stone, clear and strong, and precious as a diamond; and full against the forehead of whatever giant says that dying infants are damned, you send this answer: "*Even so it is not the will of your Father which is in heaven that one of these little ones should perish.*"

Yes, that is the simple and mighty truth. Hundreds and even thousands of learned and subtle doctors may have taught the possible perdition of infants. Poets great and small may have embalmed the doctrine in their verse, like a fly in amber or a toad in mud. But for all that it is false. The Church to-day refuses to believe it; all Christendom to-day rejects it, and casts it out.[1] You and I turn from

---

[1] Except possibly the strict Romanist (*vide* Cardinal Gibbons, " The Faith of our Fathers," pp. 310–316) and the ultra-Calvinist.

it, and deny it. And why? By what power has the heart of Christendom been strengthened to expel this doctrine? By the power of the pure Word of God overcoming the deadly logic of the schools. By what authority do we decline to believe that there is a single infant in perdition? By the authority of Jesus Christ, who has enlightened our hearts to know and trust a holy and just and loving God.

II. Come, then, and let us understand exactly where we stand upon this question, and what is the strength of our position. It is not merely an amiable repugnance to believe what is unpleasant; it is rather an absolute refusal to believe what is unscriptural and unchristian. It is not merely a protest of the affections against a harsh doctrine; it is a protest of the faith against a false doctrine. And we propose to set in order some of the reasons why we do not and will not believe it.

(1) The doctrine of the perdition of infants is false, because there is nothing

in the Word of God to support it. Search the Scriptures from beginning to end, and you will not find a single word, a single syllable, which implies that children are to be sent into everlasting death.

But some one will say, "What, then, do you make of the command which was given to the Israelites to destroy the children of Amalek? How do you explain that?" We do not explain it. We simply deny that it has anything to do with the question. For even if you admit that such a command came from God instead of from the hearts of half-enlightened men, the death of little children amid the cruelties of ancient war no more justifies us in thinking that God would cast them into perdition, than the fact that your child had burned his hand in the fire that glows on your hearth would be a proof that you were willing to shut him up in a fiery prison forever.

"But then," the objector may continue, "what do you say to the declaration that the sins of the parents shall be visited upon the children unto the third and fourth generation?" We say that you have stopped short in the middle of the quotation. For how does it read? "*The sins of the fathers upon the children unto the third and fourth generation of them that hate me.*" Only where the hatred against God continues, and works, and utters itself in wickedness, does the divine anger rest. Not upon the helpless and harmless babe, not upon the little children born in the homes of ignorance and vice; for them the good God has only the tenderest pity and compassion. The very fact that they are involved, without their fault, without their choice, in the pain and trouble of a sin-cursed world, is a mystery of hope in the darkness of their death. For out of a world in which the harmless are tangled in the net with the guilty, they pass into the presence of that God who is plenteous in mercy, and who is not willing that one of these little ones should perish. Shall He not recompense them for the brief sorrows of their mortal life? I tell you, the world to come would have no meaning, the future life would be a vain and empty delusion, if it did not contain the promise of deliverance for helpless sufferers. And I challenge any one to find a single word in the Bible which teaches that the sorrows falling upon little children in this world of sin and shame are continued for one instant after the angel of death has set their spirits free to enter the world of light.

(2) But this argument is only negative, and we must pass on at once to the second point, which is positive. The doctrine of the perdition of infants is false, because it is condemned by natural justice.

This is an argument which needs to be used with caution, and with an implicit understanding of those limitations and conditions which people of intelligence always take for granted in the simple statement of a broad and general principle. It is not to be supposed for a moment that everything which we cannot see to be right must therefore be wrong. It is not to be assumed for a moment that our human sense of justice is perfect and infallible, or that we are acquainted with all the considerations which enter into the judgment of God.

But there is, in spite of all ignorance and defect, a perception of equity in the human soul which corresponds to the attribute of righteousness in God. And this is what we affirm: the more highly this moral sense is educated, the more clearly and unequivocally does it reluctate against the notion that God will condemn the soul of one little child to everlasting death, either on account of the guilt of Adam's sin, or on account of the neglect of its parents to have it baptized.

For here, mark you, we are not considering the operations of Providence, in which there must be inscrutable mysteries, since they proceed upon general laws too large for our comprehension; nor are we discussing the methods and means of divine justice in the present transitory state of things, in which we know that the tares cannot be separated from the wheat, and in which we are conscious of suffering brought upon us by the voluntary transgression or the careless neglect of others. All that goes without saying. But now we are looking onward to the final result of the divine justice; and the one thought that enables us to submit with humility to the apparent inequalities in the course of Providence in this world, and to reconcile ourselves to the present sufferings of those who have not consciously or wilfully offended, is the firm conviction that these will all be rectified and compensated at last, and that the end of all things will manifest the equity of God in clear splendour.

In the absence, then, of any authentic revelation that infants will go into perdition, in the absence of any credible witness to inform us that he has seen "babes in hell not a span long," we assert, against all logical and theological deductions, the instinctive and inalienable sense of justice in the human heart.

> " A warmth within the breast would melt
> The freezing reason's colder part;
> And, like a man in wrath, the heart
> Stood up and answered, I have felt."

How could we believe such a morally insane doctrine as that the final outworking of God's justice will be to spare the original offender and damn his helpless children? For that, in plain language, is what it all amounts to. Adam is saved. The Church has given him a place among the saints. Raphael has painted him among the blessed who sit around the throne, in the great picture of the *Disputa della Trinita*. Dante has described him as the first in that happy circle which surrounds the mystic Rose of Paradise. From these pictures of celestial bliss we are told to cast our eyes downward and contemplate the miseries of myriads of Adam's children who have been plunged into eternal torment solely on account of his sin. The vision is a dream of madness. It is a nightmare monstrosity of error. Before I could believe in it, I should have to annihilate my conscience and commit moral suicide.

(3) But there is a still stronger argument against the perdition of infants. It is directly contrary to the principles of judgment as they are revealed to us by Jesus Christ.

Let us understand very clearly that Christ teaches that there is punishment in the future world, and that this punishment is so great that it passes the power of human thought to conceive it. But let us never forget that He teaches also that this punishment is just and righteous, and that not a single stroke of it will ever fall upon any who have not deserved it by their own sins and refused deliverance by their own impenitence. Listen to His parables of judgment, and you shall hear of men who are condemned for pride and selfishness and greed, like Dives and the unmerciful servant; you shall hear of men who are condemned for neglect of duty and contempt of God, like the man with one talent and the unfaithful steward; you shall hear of men who are condemned for hardness of heart, like those who ministered not to the sick and the hungry and the prisoners, or for scorn of mercy, like those who would not come to the wedding feast, and him who would not put on the wedding garment; you shall hear of men who are condemned for rejecting the prophets and slaying the Saviour, like the wicked husbandmen. These all pass into darkness, but it is because they have already loved darkness and lived in it. This is the very principle of their judgment, — that they have deserved it, they have brought it upon themselves. They are lost because they will not be saved, because they are cruel and rebellious and unjust and negligent and scornful. And it is for this reason that the loving and gracious Christ tells us of their perdition, in order that we may know that we also must give account to God of the deeds done in the body.

Now, if you introduce another principle of judgment, if you say that any soul may be lost for the sin of Adam, for not accepting an invitation which it could not understand, for not receiving a baptism which was never offered, for not repenting and believing before repentance and faith were possible, — if you introduce any such foreign principle, you absolutely cancel and obliterate the teachings of Christ, and leave the future world a moral chaos, dominated solely by a blind and brutal terror. If judgment means anything, it means that this is forever impossible. If the words of Christ mean anything, they mean that not one helpless, harmless child will ever be banished into the outer darkness by the just God.

(4) And this brings us to the fourth and last reason for rejecting the doctrine of infant perdition. It is false, because it is contrary to the revelation of the love of God which is given unto us in Christ Jesus our Lord. There was a time when men refused to accept this revelation in its integrity, because it would not fit into their theories. Coming to the text, "*God so loved the world*," they cut it down to suit their logic, and said, "This means the world of the elect." But by the gracious Spirit of God the darkness of that time has been dispelled. We believe that Christ meant just what He said. We believe that God is love, and that His mighty heart broods over all the world with an infinite tenderness, willing to save and bless it. Everywhere that love is flowing, following, seeking, calling for its children. Into every soul that does not refuse it, it will come. In every life that does not reject it, it will accomplish its divine purpose. And sooner shall our hearts learn

No Children Lost. 39

to forget and hate the children that have nestled beside them, sooner shall our hands be ready to cast them into the flames, than God's heart shall forget, than God's hand shall cast away, one of the little souls that pass, helpless and harmless, out of the shadow of their brief mortal life into the light of his loving presence.

And here, for to-day, we must pause. In the next sermon I shall ask you to consider the proofs that all who die in infancy are certainly saved, and that there is a heaven full of happy children. But for the present we desire to make clear, beyond all possibility of mistake, our rejection of infant perdition.

We do not believe that there are any children in hell. We acknowledge that men have taught this doctrine in the past, — men of all ages and of many churches, but we do not accept their teaching. If it is written or implied in any creed, we refuse allegiance to it. If it is an essential part of any theological system, we cut loose from it. Out of the shadow of that darkness we have emerged. And the light that has led us is not the light of our own reason, but the light of the knowledge of the glory of God shining in the face of Jesus Christ. At His manger-cradle we have learned the meaning of the Gospel for Little Children; and henceforth for us there shall come no haunting terror, no black despair, into the room where a child is dying. If we must see the dear face grow pale, and feel the little hand grow cold, at least it shall be with a spirit untroubled by any mistrust of God, with a love that is calm, and still, and secure of the future. All shall be quiet and peaceful in that last vigil of affection: —

> "We watched her breathing through the night,
>   Her breathing soft and low,
> As in her breast the wave of life
>   Kept heaving to and fro.
>
> "Our very hopes belied our fears,
>   Our fears our hopes belied;
> We thought her dying when she slept,
>   And sleeping when she died.

"For when the morn came, dim and sad,
And chill with early showers,
Her quiet eyelids closed, — she had
Another morn than ours."

Come away, then, from that still room. Close the door softly, and whisper to yourself, in the assurance of a divine faith, "*Even so it is not the will of our Father in heaven that one of these little ones should perish.*"

MY CHILD.

    I CANNOT make him dead!
    His fair sunshiny head
Is ever bounding round my study chair;
    Yet, when my eyes, now dim
    With tears, I turn to him,
The vision vanishes — he is not there!

    I walk my parlor floor,
    And, through the open door,
I hear a footfall on the chamber stair;
    I'm stepping toward the hall
    To give the boy a call;
And then bethink me that — he is not there!

    I thread the crowded street;
    A satchelled lad I meet,
With the same beaming eyes and colored hair;
    And, as he's running by,
    Follow him with my eye,
Scarcely believing that — he is not there!

    I know his face is hid
    Under the coffin-lid;
Closed are his eyes; cold is his forehead fair;

My hand that marble felt;
O'er it in prayer I knelt;
Yet my heart whispers that — he is not there!

I cannot make him dead!
When passing by the bed,
So long watched over with parental care,
My spirit and my eye
Seek him inquiringly,
Before the thought comes that — he is not there!

When, at the cool, gray break
Of day, from sleep I wake,
With my first breathing of the morning air
My soul goes up with joy,
To Him who gave my boy;
Then comes the sad thought that — he is not there!

When at the day's calm close,
Before we seek repose,
I'm with his mother, offering up our prayer;
Whate'er I may be saying,
I am in spirit praying
For our boy's spirit, though — he is not there!

Not there! Where, then, is he?
The form I used to see
Was but the raiment that he used to wear.
The grave, that now doth press
Upon that cast-off dress,
Is but his wardrobe locked; — he is not there!

He lives! — In all the past
He lives; nor, to the last,
Of seeing him again will I despair;
In dreams I see him now;
And, on his angel brow,
I see it written, "Thou shalt see me *there!*"

Yes, we all live to God!
Father, Thy chastening rod
So help us, thine afflicted ones, to bear,
That, in the spirit-land,
Meeting at Thy right hand,
'T will be our heaven to find that — he is there!

JOHN PIERPONT.

All Children Saved

II.

Suffer the little children to come unto me, and forbid them not; for of such is the kingdom of God. — Mark x. 14.

WE have good reason for refusing to believe that God would send the soul of a little child into endless punishment. If we attach any meaning to the words "just" and "merciful," as we use them in speaking of the Divine Being, they imply a character in God which must make it impossible for Him to deal thus with the most helpless of His creatures. It would be contrary to the nature of God as He is revealed in Jesus Christ. It would destroy the foundation principles of the divine judgment as they are laid down in the New Testament. It would sweep away the very grounds on which we accept the Bible as the Word of God, and the reasons which lead us to worship and love our Father in heaven. For surely the strongest arguments in favour of Christianity are those which are addressed to our moral sense. It appeals to us most deeply because it answers the purest and highest instincts of our nature, — instincts of justice, of compassion, of goodness, of love. And so long as we rely upon these to support the claims of Christianity, we are entitled — or rather we are bound — to rely upon them to interpret the teachings of Christianity.

It is upon these moral instincts, then, that we fall back in our rejection of the horrible decree of infant perdition. No logical deductions from the human statement of theological premises can force us to accept a conclusion so repugnant to the moral sense. On the contrary, such deductions amount simply to a disproof of the principles from which they are drawn. They act as a *reductio ad absurdum;* and

All Children Saved. 51

we refuse to believe either the dogma that there is no salvation without baptism, or the dogma that an absolute and eternal decree foreordains men to be damned, simply because these dogmas would lead to the conclusion that there are babes in hell, and so destroy our faith in the ultimate justice and goodness of God.

But you see at once that this attitude is altogether negative. It sets us free from the falsehood, but it does not put us in possession of the truth. "Remorse of equity," as Hooker has called it, had driven many a man into this position even in the days when the doctrine of infant perdition was taught in its unmitigated severity, and when the rejection of it involved the peril of condemnation for heresy.

Michael Servetus was one of these. Among the errors for which the magistrates of Geneva condemned him to be burned was this: he taught that "all who are taken from life as infants and children are exempt from eternal death." And I think you will agree with me that this particular heresy was one for which a man could suffer martyrdom with honour. Episcopius also, the leader of the Arminians, held that infants are liberated by special divine grace from the perdition of sin. Hugo Grotius, the first and the greatest of modern lawyers, uttered his clear protest against the horrible decree which consigns helpless children to inevitable perdition.

Many others took the same ground; some of them were avowedly Calvinists, but they held that Calvin was not infallible, and refused to follow him beyond the Word of God. Among them was a man whose name is familiar to all of us, — Dr. Isaac Watts, the poet, whose " Little Busy Bee" still serves as an example to good children, and whose hymns we still sing with love in our churches. He professed himself utterly unwilling to believe that " any little children are condemned to eternal misery for nothing else but because they were born of Adam, the original transgressor." But, not being able to see his way beyond this denial, he boldly cut the Gordian knot of their destiny by affirming his opinion that many of them at death are annihilated, and pass out of existence altogether. It was a daring conclusion, and yet infinitely wiser and more reasonable than the doctrine of Saint Augustine or Calvin.

But is it indeed the final word upon the subject? Is it not possible for those who hold fast to the Bible as the Word of God, and believe in Jesus Christ as the Saviour of the world, to go far beyond the denial that there are infants in hell?

Surely that is only the first step in the path that leads out of the darkness into the light. The same principles that justify us in believing that the little children are not of the kingdom of Satan, give us the assurance that they belong to the kingdom of God. Nay, more; we have " a more sure word of prophecy" for this sermon than we had for the first. There we met the false logic of men with arguments drawn from our own moral nature in its response to the teachings of the Scripture; but here we bring the importunate question of the heart in regard to the future state of little children directly to the gospel of Jesus Christ for an answer.

I will admit that without this gospel we should be in the dark. Justice alone does not demand the *salvation* of little children. But mercy — mercy of God as it is revealed in Jesus — does assure their salvation. Far, and infinitely far beyond the best intimations that natural religion and the moral sense can give us, — yes, far beyond a submissive willingness to leave the fate of infants in the hands of that God whose tender mercies are over all his works,[1] and far beyond the pious hope that they will be saved,[2] — we follow

[1] Sermons by President Dickinson of Princeton, p. 205.
[2] Dr. Archibald Alexander's letter to Bishop Meade of Virginia, 1849.

the spirit of the gospel and the teachings of Jesus Christ to affirm our faith that all who die in infancy are saved, and that there is a heaven full of happy children.

I propose to-day to set in order some of the grounds on which that faith rests; so that when any one asks, "What becomes of little children when they die?" we may understand that we have a right to answer positively, "They are all saved."

And first of all, let us mention with honour the names of some of the great and good men of the past who have held this faith and expressed it under difficulties. Ulrich Zwingle, the brave Swiss reformer, who died at the head of his followers, fighting for liberty of conscience, was one. Isaac Barrow, the learned English mathematician and theologian, was another. Augustus Toplady, whose noble hymn, "Rock of Ages," is a joy forever to the Church, was another. Lyman Beecher, who stood like a bulwark against infidelity in our country during the first half of this century, was another. And, not to weary you with the noble names which now come rushing in upon us in the full tide of a "larger hope," Charles Hodge, — venerable and beloved man, for whose instructions and example I thank God as one of the greatest blessings of my life, — Charles Hodge, pillar of orthodoxy and defender of the faith, was another of those who affirmed their belief in the salvation of all who die in infancy. Before he passed to his reward in heaven, he bore testimony that "the common doctrine of evangelical Protestants is that all who die in infancy are saved."

Mark these words. It is not an individual opinion, which you and I hold in opposition to our brethren. It is not a secret desire which we cherish without reason or Scripture to sustain it. It is a common doctrine, which we hold in the brotherhood of the faith and preach as a part of the blessed gospel. The man who does not hold it is a modern heretic, a separatist, a solitary, a belated wanderer out of the Dark Ages, a man born three centuries behind his time, a man like the demoniac of Gadara, whose dwelling is among the tombs,—a man who knows not "the things that have come to pass in these days." For the hidden hope that sprang up in the hearts of a few disciples in the past, forcing its way like a trickling stream through the crevices of those massive walls of logic which were built to dam it down, has been fed by the Word of God and the Spirit of Christ until it has risen into the flood of a mighty river, sweeping the ponderous barriers away like chaff.

No progress in theology? Yes, thank God, there is progress. Not greater or more divine was the advance when Saint Paul vindicated the right of the Gentiles to a place in the kingdom of Christ; not greater or more divine was the advance when Luther and Calvin and Knox broke the chains of Roman error, and gave the Church the open Bible as her inheritance;

not greater or more divine was any step that the Church of Christ has ever taken, than that which lies between the days when venerable doctors of the Westminster Assembly believed that God was glorified by many children of Turks and Indians crying and leaping in hell, and this day, in which we affirm our common evangelical faith that all dying infants are saved, and that God's heaven is thronged with happy children.

But why do we believe this, and on what ground do we teach it? Let us state the reasons for our faith as briefly and as simply as possible.

1. In the first place, we believe in the salvation of all the little children, because we believe that Jesus Christ died for all mankind. It was the world that God loved in His infinite compassion, and it was to take away the sin of the world that God sent His own Son to live a perfect life and to taste death for every man upon the cross of Calvary. This is the teaching of

the Holy Scripture. To narrow or confine it is to do dishonour to the Word of God; nay, worse, it is to tie the hands that were pierced upon the cross with the bonds of our theology.

The atonement of Jesus Christ has an infinite value and a world-wide meaning. It has a relation to the whole human race; not merely a possible relation, a theoretical relation, but an actual relation. It is bestowed upon all mankind, as the air we breathe, as the sun that shines on us. It is a universal gift. It is the light which lighteth every man that cometh into the world.

Why is it, then, that all men do not receive its benefits? Simply and solely because they will not. "Ye will not come to me," said Jesus, "that ye might have life."[1]

And who are they whose lives are unblessed, whose souls are unsaved by Jesus Christ? Only those of whom the Scrip-

[1] John v. 40.

ture clearly tells us that they have no part in His kingdom; those who walk in pride and hardness of heart, unwilling to repent and seek mercy at God's hand; those who walk in iniquity, following their fleshly lusts; those who walk in darkness because they hate light; those who walk in cruelty and oppression because they despise their fellow-men; those who turn away from Jesus Christ and count the blood of the everlasting covenant an unholy thing, — these are they who shall never enter into the Holy City, nor find a place in God's blessed kingdom.

But by what right, by what authority of Scripture, by what sanction of Jesus Christ would you cast out one little child to dwell among those wicked ones? What reason would God have for refusing admittance to one little child who knocked at heaven's gate? Christ died for all; and His death avails for all except those whom the Gospel itself excludes from its benefits. There is not a line or a word to shut out one of the little dying children. Therefore Christ died for them, and Christ saves them when they die.

But perhaps some one will say, "How, then, do you get rid of the consequences of the Fall? How do you explain away the guilt of original sin which rests upon every descendant of the guilty Adam?" We do not explain it away. We are willing to accept the very strongest statement of it that you can possibly draw from the Bible; and the stronger you make it, the more clearly does it prove the salvation of infants. For not one word does the Scripture say of the relation of Adam to the race, which it does not say of the relation of Christ to the race. If Adam was the federal head of a fallen humanity, then Christ was the federal head of a redeemed humanity. If Adam's transgression brought a curse on all mankind, then Christ's atonement brought a blessing upon all mankind. The closer you bind a child to his fallen Father Adam, the closer do you bind him to his risen Father Christ. If it is true that

> "In Adam's fall
> We sinned all,"

it is just as true that

> "Christ Jesu's cross
> Redeem'd our loss."

Turn to the fifth chapter of the Epistle to the Romans, and read what the inspired Apostle Paul has written on this subject. It is an immense gospel, wider than the earth and deeper than the sea: "So then as through one trespass the judgment came unto all men to condemnation, even so through one act of righteousness the free gift came unto all men to justification of life. For as through one man's disobedience the many were made sinners, even so through the obedience of one shall the many be made righteous."[1] What interpretation can we put upon this language? What in the name of truth and honesty can it mean, unless it means that

[1] Romans v. 18, 19.

the obedience of Christ countervails the disobedience of Adam, and blots it out completely? Yes, that is the doctrine of Scripture. Original sin is all atoned for; the guilt of it is taken away forever from the race by the Lamb of God. No living soul shall ever perish for Adam's transgression. "For if by the trespass of one the many died, much more did the grace of God, and the gift by the grace of the one man Jesus Christ, abound unto the many."[1]

The little child that comes into the world is born into a sinful humanity, but it is not guilty in God's sight any more than it is guilty in your sight. It is made innocent by the precious blood of Christ, as of a lamb without spot or blemish; and if it passes out of this world before it has wilfully turned away from the mercy of God, before it has chosen sin and loved it and lived in it, it passes pure and guiltless, a ransomed spirit, a lost child found,

[1] Romans v. 15.

a beloved child saved, into the boundless love of our Father in heaven.

2. In the second place, we believe in the salvation of all dying infants, because it is in accordance with the teachings of Christianity in regard to the desire and purpose of God to save every soul that can possibly be saved, and the vast extent of His kingdom of eternal happiness.

These teachings are not confined to the New Testament. We find them embedded in the prophecies which foretold the coming of Christ. No one can read the Bible candidly without acknowledging that it tells from the very beginning of a God that delighteth not in the death of the wicked, — a God that loveth mercy and findeth in judgment a strange work. Christ came into this world to reveal this God, — to show us the very heart of His heart and the abundance of His love. And the Apostles of Christ proclaimed Him as a God not willing that any should perish.

Now, think for a moment of the presence and power of His Holy Spirit, who worketh where and when and how He pleaseth, — as secret and as viewless as "the wind that bloweth where it listeth, and thou canst not tell whence it cometh and whither it goeth," — think of that Spirit of life and love moving silently everywhere through the world, and imagine, if you can, that the souls of little children whom God loves, whom God desires to save, are lost to Him as they flutter through the gates of death into the other world. Shall it be said of the sparrows that "not one of them · falleth to the ground without your Father," and yet shall the flocks of childish souls fly away into the night without His notice or His care? I tell you, not one of those little wanderers can slip unseen past the good Father who watches and waits for them.

Is there any spiritual grace which they require to fit them for the vision of God? The Spirit can bestow that grace upon them, even though they are unconscious of it. Do they need to be born again? He who gave them life will give them new life. They fly from our arms, not into the arms of darkness, but into the arms of God; and with Him they are safe.

If this were not true, how, then, should we understand the teachings of the Bible in regard to the immense number of the redeemed, and the measureless population of the city of God? Out of our human race the vast majority perish in childhood. And yet the promise of God has ever been that the company of the redeemed should far exceed the company of the lost. "Thy seed," said He to the father of the faithful, "shall be like the sands of the seashore. Thy seed shall be like the stars of heaven for multitude." Countless myriads, more than the human mind can number, shall be gathered in the abode of peace. The kingdom of darkness is a lake, bounded and shut in on every side; the kingdom of light is a sea, stretching far beyond our sight, and dazzling with radiance,

All Children Saved. 67

into the horizon which is infinite. The voice of death is but a slender note vanishing in the night; the voice of praise is as the sound of many waters rising forever about the throne of God and the Lamb.

> "Ten thousand times ten thousand,
> In sparkling raiment bright,
> The armies of the ransomed saints
> Throng up the steeps of light."

And how shall that ever be, how shall the number of the redeemed immeasurably surpass the number of the lost, unless that great, silent, helpless majority of the human race who die in childhood shall be gathered among the blessed in God's kingdom? In those mighty throngs there will be countless little saints, born in pain on earth for a moment that they might live in joy in heaven forever. In that vast anthem of increasing praise there will be a part set for children's voices,— a part that none could sing save those whose only music had been learned from the angels.

Do you remember Raphael's picture — the Sistine Madonna? The cloud against which the holy child Jesus and his mother are revealed seems at first sight to be only a celestial vapour; but as you look at it more closely you see that it is composed of beautiful, shining infant faces. It is no poet's dream; it is a reality. The very air of heaven is populous and radiant with happy childhood. That which the prophet wrote in his ancient vision of the earthly Jerusalem is true of the City of God: "The streets of the city shall be full of boys and girls playing in the streets thereof."

3. In the third place, we believe that all little children pass through the door of death into the heaven of God, because Jesus Christ has taught us that they belong to heaven. Hearken to His words: —

"At the same time came the disciples unto Jesus, saying, Who is the greatest in the kingdom of heaven?

"And Jesus called a little child unto him, and set him in the midst of them,

"And said, Verily, I say unto you, Except ye be converted, and become as little children, ye shall not enter into the kingdom of heaven.

"Whosoever therefore shall humble himself as this little child, the same is greatest in the kingdom of heaven.

"Take heed that ye despise not one of these little ones: for I say unto you, That in heaven their angels do always behold the face of my Father which is in heaven."[1]

"And he sat down, and called the twelve, and saith unto them, If any man desire to be first, the same shall be last of all, and servant of all.

"And he took a child, and set him in the midst of them: and when he had taken him in his arms, he said unto them,

"Whosoever shall receive one of such children in my name, receiveth me: and whosoever shall receive me, receiveth not me, but him that sent me."[2]

"And they brought young children to him, that he should touch them: and his disciples rebuked those that brought them.

[1] Matt. xviii. 1-4, 10.   [2] Mark ix. 35-37.

"But when Jesus saw it, he was much displeased, and said unto them, Suffer the little children to come unto me, and forbid them not: for of such is the kingdom of God.

"Verily I say unto you, Whosoever shall not receive the kingdom of God as a little child, he shall not enter therein.

"And he took them up in his arms, put his hands upon them, and blessed them."[1]

I have said that our Master taught that the little children belong to heaven. It is, indeed, too little to claim for His teaching. For, as we look more closely at that fourteenth verse of the tenth chapter of St. Mark, we see that the words "of such" stand in the original in the genitive of possession. And this is the glorious truth that leaps out to meet us: "The kingdom of God *belongs* to such." It is the children's inheritance, their possession, their kingdom. Not one soul shall ever enter it who does not come as a little child, nor shall one who comes as a child fail to obtain an entrance.

[1] Mark x. 13-16.

With these gracious words we may rest our case; and so we come to the end of our two sermons on the state of little children after death. It is a task that has been before my mind through many months. I have studied and longed and prayed for strength and opportunity to accomplish it, — to proclaim clearly, and to prove certainly out of the Word of God, that there is not a single infant in hell, and that heaven is thronged with happy children. And if any one shall ask why I have cared so much about this, and taken so much pains and time to do it, let me give him a simple and straightforward answer.

It was not for the sake of casting any reproach upon those teachers of the past who have failed to read this doctrine in the Bible. It would be a strange thing if we could not reverence the wise and good men who have gone before us, even while we recognize that they were finite and fallible. It would be a strange thing if we could not cling to the heritage of truth which they have left us, all the more firmly because we do not hesitate to purify it from the errors of a deceptive human logic. If we see a little farther into the Bible than they did, it is not by our own light, but by the illumination which God gives like the growing day; and that should never make us proud, but humble and grateful, and willing always to wait upon the Spirit of the Lord.

Nor was it for the sake of making you think less of the justice and sovereignty of God that I desired to preach these sermons. On the contrary, it was to make you think more of those great doctrines, and to think of them not blindly, but with open eyes. God is infinitely just, and therefore the same judgment which condemns you and me for the evil that we have done, justifies and saves the little child that has never done evil. God is absolutely sovereign, and therefore He can and will save all those who do not despise and reject his mercy.

But there were just three reasons why my heart was constrained and mightily impelled to preach this gospel about children.

First, in order to make it easier for you to love God. If any one of you has ever thought of him as an impassive, supreme, iron-willed Monarch whose arbitrary decree sends immortal souls to death or to life solely and equally for His own good pleasure and glory, banish that thought forever from your mind. Learn to think of Him as the great Father whose nature and whose name is Love. Even as the sunlight embraces and encircles the whole earth, so does His love embrace and encircle all humanity. Night comes only when we turn away from it; day comes when we turn toward it. It is our duty to love God because everything in Him is supremely and perfectly lovable. That is salvation, — to love God and our fellow-men even as He loves us. And surely if anything can help us to do that, it is the thought of His infinite, unceasing, everlasting care and tenderness for the little children who suffer and die on earth.

The second reason why I have longed to preach this truth to you is in order that it might lead and draw you upward into a better life. There are some of you whose little children have been taken away into a happier world; and yet you are still living without God and without hope, living in sin and impenitence, living without a personal faith in Jesus Christ or an open acceptance of Him as your Saviour. Oh that the memories of human love might bring you into the kingdom of the divine love! that you might be called by a still, small voice — the voice of a little child — out of a careless, sinful life into the life that leads to heaven! that you might learn to say with David, "I shall go to him, though he may not return to me!" Then, indeed, you would come, penitent and heart-broken, to the feet of Jesus, and cry, "Lord, thou art the Good Shepherd of my little lamb; be also the Shepherd of my soul forever, and bring us together in thy heavenly fold."

There is one more reason why I have longed to preach and prove to you the salvation of the little children. It is for consolation and comfort. The Gospel of Jesus Christ is not sad tidings; it is glad tidings. It is sent to bind up the broken-hearted, to give them the oil of joy for mourning, and the spirit of praise for the garment of heaviness. If there is any place where we need this comfort, it is at the death-bed of little children. To see them suffer, — so timid, so frail, so helpless; unable to express their pain, or tell us what we can do to aid them; and yet often so brave in their silent, childish heroism, — that tries our courage and our faith even to the uttermost. There is nothing that can sustain us, there is nothing that can console and quiet us, when the bright presence has vanished, and the little voice is still, save the thought that God has taken His own again, and that the brief sorrow is changed into an eternal joy.

"There is a Reaper, whose name is Death,
    And with his sickle keen
He reaps the bearded grain at a breath,
    And the flowers that grow between.

. . . .

"He gazed at the flowers with tearful eyes,
    He kissed their drooping leaves;
It was for the Lord of Paradise
    He bound them in his sheaves.

"'My Lord has need of these flowerets gay,'
    The Reaper said, and smiled;
'Dear tokens of the earth are they
    Where he was once a child.'

. . . .

"And the mother gave, in tears and pain,
    The flowers she most did love;
She knew she should find them all again
    In the fields of light above.

"Oh, not in cruelty, not in wrath,
    The Reaper came that day;
'T was an angel visited the green earth,
    And took the flowers away."

THE THREE SONS.

I HAVE a son, a little son, a boy just five years old,
With eyes of thoughtful earnestness, and mind of gentle mould.
They tell me that unusual grace in all his ways appears,
That my child is grave and wise of heart beyond his childish years.
I cannot say how this may be; I know his face is fair —
And yet his chiefest comeliness is his sweet and serious air;
I know his heart is kind and fond; I know he loveth me;
But loveth yet his mother more with grateful fervency.
But that which others most admire, is the thought which fills his mind,
The food for grave inquiring speech he everywhere doth find.
Strange questions doth he ask of me, when we together walk;
He scarcely thinks as children think, or talks as children talk.

Nor cares he much for childish sports, dotes not on bat or ball,
But looks on manhood's ways and works, and aptly mimics all.
His little heart is busy still, and oftentimes perplext
With thoughts about this world of ours, and thoughts about the next.
He kneels at his dear mother's knee; she teacheth him to pray;
And strange, and sweet, and solemn then are the words which he will say.
Oh, should my gentle child be spared to manhood's years like me,
A holier and a wiser man I trust that he will be;
And when I look into his eyes, and stroke his thoughtful brow,
I dare not think what I should feel, were I to lose him now.

I have a son, a second son, a simple child of three;
I 'll not declare how bright and fair his little features be,
How silver sweet those tones of his when he prattles on my knee;
I do not think his light-blue eye is, like his brother's keen,
Nor his brow so full of childish thought as his hath ever been;

But his little heart's a fountain pure of kind and
    tender feeling;
And his every look's a gleam of light, rich depths
    of love revealing.
When he walks with me, the country folk, who pass
    us in the street,
Will shout for joy, and bless my boy, he looks so
    mild and sweet.
A playfellow he is to all; and yet, with cheerful tone
Will sing his little song of love, when left to sport
    alone.
His presence is like sunshine sent to gladden home
    and hearth,
To comfort us in all our griefs, and sweeten all our
    mirth.
Should he grow up to riper years, God grant his
    heart may prove
As sweet a home for heavenly grace as now for
    earthly love.
And if, beside his grave, the tears of aching eyes
    must dim,
God comfort us for all the love which we shall lose
    in him.

I have a son, a third sweet son; his age I cannot
    tell,
For they reckon not by years and months where he
    has gone to dwell.
To us, for fourteen anxious months, his infant
    smiles were given;

And then he bade farewell to Earth, and went to
    live in Heaven.
I cannot tell what form is his, what looks he weareth now,
Nor guess how bright a glory crowns his shining
    seraph brow.
The thoughts that fill his sinless soul, the bliss
    which he doth feel,
Are numbered with the secret things which God
    will not reveal.
But I know (for God hath told me this) that he is
    now at rest,
Where other blessed infants be, on their Saviour's
    loving breast :
I know his spirit feels no more this weary load of
    flesh,
But his sleep is blessed with endless dreams of joy
    forever fresh.
I know the angels fold him close beneath their glittering wings,
And soothe him with a song that breathes of Heaven's divinest things.
I know that we shall meet our babe (his mother
    dear and I)
Where God for aye shall wipe away all tears from
    every eye.
Whate'er befalls his brethren twain, his bliss can
    never cease;
Their lot may here be grief and fear, but his is
    certain peace.

It may be that the tempter's wiles their souls from
   bliss may sever;
But, if our own poor faith fail not, he must be ours
   forever.
When we think of what our darling is, and what we
   still must be —
When we muse on that world's perfect bliss, and
   this world's misery —
When we groan beneath this load of sin, and feel
   this grief and pain —
Oh, we'd rather lose our other two, than have him
   here again!

JOHN MOULTRIE.

THE END.

www.ingramcontent.com/pod-product-compliance
Lightning Source LLC
Chambersburg PA
CBHW020324090426
42735CB00009B/1396